The Unofficial Wizard's Cocktail Book

100+ Extraordinary Cocktail Recipes Inspired by the Magic Films

Margie Valadez

Table of Contents

Introduction 5
   Luscious Lemonade 6
   Wizarding Gillywater 6
   Felix Felicis ("Liquid Luck") 7
   Pureblood Mocktail 7
   A Goblet of Fire 8
   Perfect Pina Colada 8
   Flaming Dragon's Blood Mocktail 9
   Butterbeer Martinis 9
   Dragon's Blood Punch 10
   Werewolf Potion 10
   Happy Elf Mocktail 10
   The Phoenix Feather 11
   Head of Cerberus 11
   Unicorn's Blood 12
   Wizard's Butterbeer 12
   Love Potion Punch 13
   Dragon's Heart Mocktail 13
   Silver-Blue Unicorn's Blood 14
   Arch Enemy Mocktail I 14
   Arch Enemy Mocktail II 15
   Polyjuice Potion 15
   Blood-Sucking Bat Mocktail 16
   The Dark Wizard Mocktail 16
   Just the Tonic 17
   Black Lemonade 17
   Black Magic Mocktail 18
   Blood Mocktail 18
   "Bourbon" Butterbeer 19
   Bloody Mary Mocktail 19
   Pumpkin Mocktail 20
   Lizard Skin Mocktail 20
   Witches Blood Brew 21
   Witches Brew Punch 21
   Elderflower Wand Apple Martini 22
   Under the Tequila Sunrise 22
   Twisted Espresso Martini 23
   Bewitched Blueberry Mojito 23
   Beastly Black Russian 24
   Bergamot Mystical Mojito 24

Wizard's Hat Coco Fizz 25
Supernatural Sloe Gin 25
Captivating Zucchini Martini 26
Mischievous Mai Tai 26
Dreamy Driver's Punch 27
Potent Peach Punch 27
Vodka and Cranberry Blush 28
Whispering Walnut Old Fashioned 28
Sorcerer's Strawberry Daiquiri 29
Brilliant Blue Hawaiian 29
Gleeful Grasshopper Cocktail 30
Wonderous White Russian 30
Wonderful Watermelon Margaritas 31
Captivating Caribbean Breeze 31
Beguiling Beer Margaritas 32
Mesmerizing Mimosa 32
Abracadabra Baybreeze Cocktail 33
Saints and Sinners 33
Prickly Pear Cactus Margarita 34
Marvelous Mangorita 34
Scrumptious Screwrita 35
Captivating Classic Daiquiri 35
Ramos Gin Fizz 36
Frothing Boston Sour 36
Tantalizing Tom Collins Cocktail 37
Naughty New York Sour 37
Mystical Moscow Mule 38
Celebratory Champagne Cocktail 38
Apprentice's Aperol Spritz 39
Charming Gin and Tonic 39
Conjurer's Cosmopolitan Cocktail 40
Perfect Amaretto Sour 40
Perfect Pomegranate Martini 41
Pretty Paloma Cocktail 41
Classic Sidecar Cocktail 42
Genius Gin Gimlet 42
Pickled Pepper Potion 43

Conclusion 44

Appendix Measurement Conversion Chart... 45

Introduction

This book is a fantastic way to immerse yourself in the world of wizards and magic without needing complicated or advanced culinary skills. The recipes included in this book will help you create delicious potions, drinks, and mocktails that will leave everyone spellbound.
Whether you're preparing these recipes on your own or organizing a party for your fellow wizards, this book is a must-have to set the right mood.
All you need are this book, a few simple ingredients, and the right equipment. (Wizard's hat and wand are optional.) We hope you have lots of fun creating some magic in your very own kitchen.

Luscious Lemonade

This lemonade is the perfect combination of sweet and sour—ideal for a hot summer's evening after a day spent mixing potions and casting spells!

Prep Time: 5 minutes
Servings: 1

Ingredients:
- 1¼ ounces lemon juice
- ¾ ounces simple syrup
- 4 ounces club soda, chilled
- Sugar
- Ice cubes

Directions:
1. Make a tiny pile of sugar on a plate. Using a lemon, moisten the rim of a glass. Dip the rim of the glass in the sugar, making sure it is well covered.
2. Add the ice cubes, simple syrup, and lemon juice to a shaker. For 20 seconds, mix the ingredients together.
3. Pour the mixture into a glass and top with the club soda.

Notes: Garnish with lemon peel or anything else appeals to you.

Wizarding Gillywater

Gillywater is made up of normal water and Gillyweed (a magical plant). When you eat Gillyweed, you grow a temporary set of gills, allowing you to breathe underwater. It also helps you swim by creating webbing between your fingers and toes.

Prep Time: 1 hour
Servings: 15

Ingredients:
- 1-gallon water (filtered or mineral)
- 1 English cucumber, washed and spiralized
- 3 sprigs fresh mint
- ½ lemon, juiced
- Ice cubes

Directions:
1. Combine all the ingredients in a large pitcher.
2. Set aside for 1 hour in the refrigerator.
3. Pour into glasses and top with cucumber slices for decoration.

Notes: The longer you allow the mixture to infuse, the stronger the flavor.

Felix Felicis ("Liquid Luck")

Felix Felicis, often known as "Liquid Luck," is a potion that makes the person who drinks it lucky for a set amount of time. The drink looks like molten gold with enormous drops leaping from its surface like goldfish, never spilling. All of the guzzler's endeavors tend to prosper until the potion's effects wear off.

Prep Time: 5 minutes
Servings: 1
Ingredients:
- 1 can lemon or lime soda
- ¼ cup orange juice
- ¼ cup lemon juice
- 1 teaspoon vanilla essence
- 1 teaspoon sugar
- Edible golden sprinkles

Directions:
1. Combine the orange juice and soda in a bowl.
2. Combine the lemon juice, sugar, and vanilla extract in a small cup.
3. Pour the lemon-vanilla mixture into the bowl. Mix well.
4. Pour into a tall glass and sprinkle the edible sprinkles on top.
5. Chill the drink in the refrigerator before serving.

Notes: Alternatively, combine the ingredients in a saucepan over medium heat and whisk until the liquid begins to boil and the sugar melts, resulting in a gold color and slightly thicker consistency.

Pureblood Mocktail

Whether you were born into a wizarding family or had to study the art of wizardry, this mocktail is for you. Cheers!

Prep Time: 5 minutes
Servings: 6

Ingredients:
- 6 ounces lemonade
- 4½ ounces blackcurrant cordial
- 12 ounces water
- Purple food coloring
- 8 ounces sugar

Directions:
1. Fill a pitcher halfway with water and stir in some food coloring until the desired color is achieved. After each drop of food coloring, vigorously stir.
2. Pour the colored water into an ice cube tray and freeze until firm.
3. In a large bowl, combine 8 ounces white sugar and 14 teaspoon food coloring and stir until well combined.
4. Use the colored sugar to coat the rims of your serving glasses. Add a couple of the colored ice cubes to each glass.
5. In a large pitcher, combine the lemonade, blackcurrant cordial, and water; pour into the glasses.

A Goblet of Fire

You'll make an awesome impression if you place the finished drink inside a smoking cloche while serving it.

Prep Time: 5 minutes
Servings: 1

Ingredients:
- 2 ounces strong-brewed barley tea (chilled)
- 1 teaspoon fresh lime juice
- 1 teaspoon fresh lemon juice
- 1 orange peel
- 2 sugar cubes
- A dash of blue food coloring
- 1 rosemary sprig

Directions:
1. Scrub the rim of a glass with the orange peel.
2. Pour all the ingredients apart from the rosemary into the glass. Stir until the sugar is completely dissolved.
3. Garnish with the rosemary.
4. Serve and enjoy!

Perfect Pina Colada

This drink is adored by wizards, fairies, witches, and humans alike.

Prep Time: 5 minutes
Servings: 3

Ingredients:
- 2 cups unsweetened pineapple juice
- ¾ cup unsweetened coconut milk
- 2 tablespoons brown sugar
- Ice cubes
- Pineapple wedges, for garnish
- Maraschino cherries, for garnish

Directions:
1. Combine the pineapple juice, coconut milk, and brown sugar in a blender.
2. Add enough ice cubes to bring the juice up to the desired level. Blend for 30 seconds or until completely smooth.
3. Pour into glasses, adding the pineapple wedges and maraschino cherries as garnish.

Notes: Fill the glasses with crushed ice to chill them while blending the juice. Before pouring the pina colada, empty the crushed ice.

Flaming Dragon's Blood Mocktail

The ultimate wizard's companion—a magnificent dragon—is the inspiration behind this incredible cocktail. I like to serve this cocktail with a garnish of raspberries or a piece of pineapple.

Prep time: 5 minutes
Servings: 1

Ingredients:
For the blood syrup:
- 12 ounces frozen raspberries
- 3 sprigs thyme
- 4 ounces white sugar
- 4 ounces water
- Red food coloring

For the mocktail:
- 2 fluid ounces apple juice
- 1½ ounces blood orange syrup
- ¾ ounce lemon juice
- 2 ice cubes
- ⅛ teaspoon red color dust
- ⅛ ounce white grape juice

Directions:
Blood Syrup
1. In a saucepan over medium-high heat, combine the raspberries, thyme, white sugar, and water.
2. Bring to a boil, stirring regularly, until the sugar has dissolved and the raspberries are soft.
3. Turn off the heat and allow the mixture to cool to room temperature. Pour the syrup into a sealable container after passing it through a fine-mesh filter. Place in the refrigerator.

Mocktail
1. In a cocktail shaker, combine the apple juice, blood orange syrup, lemon juice, ice cubes, red color dust, and grape juice. Shake for roughly 5 seconds before straining into a cocktail glass.
2. Place a spoon on the glass's surface and layer the blood syrup on top.

Butterbeer Martinis

These butterbeer martinis are amazing when served with butterscotch squares on the rim of the glass. For a sweeter taste, substitute 7-Up for Sprite.

Prep Time: 5 minutes
Servings: 1

Ingredients:
- 3 ounces root beer
- 1 teaspoon vanilla extract
- 1 teaspoon butterscotch extract
- 4 ounces cream soda
- 2 ounces Sprite

Directions:
1. In a shaker with ice, combine all the ingredients and mix for 20 seconds, or until cooled.
2. Strain the liquid into a cocktail glass and drink up!

Dragon's Blood Punch

Dragon's blood is utilized in various potions and other beneficial concoctions. If it's bottled, it's rather expensive to buy. So that's why it's a great idea to make it yourself!

Prep Time: 5 minutes
Servings: 20

Ingredients:
- 46 ounces red punch (preferably Hawaiian)
- 46 ounces apple juice
- 48 ounces cranberry juice
- 2 liters ginger ale
- 1 cup water
- Ice cubes

Directions:
1. In a large punch bowl or pot, combine all of the ingredients.
2. Stir in the ice.
3. Pour the mixture into serving glasses.

Werewolf Potion

With this delectable potion, you avoid being turned into a werewolf while also throwing a fantastic party. For a spicier flavor, try using root beer.

Prep Time: 5 minutes
Servings: 1

Ingredients:
- 1½ ounces apple juice
- 1½ ounces Worcestershire sauce
- Coca-Cola, to taste

Directions:
1. In a shaker with ice, combine the apple juice and Worcestershire sauce and mix for 20 seconds, or until chilled.
2. Strain the liquid into a glass filled with ice and cola.

Happy Elf Mocktail

House elves are hardworking characters, if not a bit on the mischievous side at times. And that's what this mocktail is like, naughty but nice. Enjoy!

Prep Time: 5 minutes
Servings: 1

Ingredients:
- 2 ounces lemonade
- 1-ounce watermelon juice
- 1-ounce white cranberry juice
- Maraschino cherries

Directions:
1. Fill a cocktail shaker halfway with ice, then add all of the ingredients.
2. Shake vigorously until well blended. Pour the mocktail into a glass and garnish it with a maraschino cherry.

The Phoenix Feather

You'll offer your cocktailing abilities to make this amazing mixture at your next party, just as the phoenix provides feathers to make magic wands. This drink has a nice tangy flavor from the grapefruit juice.

Prep Time: 5 minutes
Servings: 1

Ingredients:
- 2 ounces chamomile tea, chilled
- 1½ ounces orange juice
- 1-ounce fresh grapefruit juice
- Club soda, to taste

Directions:
1. In a shaker with ice, combine all ingredients except the club soda and shake for 20 seconds until chilled.
2. Strain the liquid into a Collins glass filled with ice and a splash of club soda.

Head of Cerberus

This drink is named after the monstrous dog of the underworld. But that's where the similarities end. Your guests will be thrilled to have this served to them. However, handle the peppers with care, and don't touch your eyes or lips until you've washed them.

Prep Time: 5 minutes
Servings: 2

Ingredients:
- ½ ounce fresh lemon juice
- 3 dashes tomato juice
- 6 ounces tonic water
- 2 slices of chili pepper
- 2 lemon wedges

Directions:
1. In a cocktail shaker with ice, all the ingredients except for the lemon wedges and chili pepper.
2. Strain the mixture into two cocktail glasses and add the lemon wedges and chili pepper on top.

Unicorn's Blood

Add dry ice to the drink at the same time as the raspberry puree for smoke if you want it to have a more magical effect. Make sure you don't put your hands on the ice.

Prep Time: 15 minutes
Servings: 2

Ingredients:
For the raspberry puree
- 7 ounces fresh raspberries
- Powdered sugar, to taste
- 2 ounces water

For the shimmer:
- 8 ounces peach juice
- 4 ounces simple syrup
- ¼ teaspoon edible gold dust
- A pinch of purple luster petal dust

Directions:
1. Puree the raspberries in a food processor. If necessary, add some water.
2. Remove the seeds from the raspberries by pressing the raspberries through a fine-mesh sieve into a bowl.
3. Gradually add 12 ounces of powdered sugar. Refrigerate until ready to use.
4. Combine the peach juice, syrup, and edible gold dust in a mixing bowl. More gold dust can be added until the desired shimmer effect is achieved. Refrigerate until ready to use.
5. Line the rim of two cocktail glasses with the purple dust. Divide the peach juice mixture between the two glasses, followed by the raspberry puree. Sprinkle with some more of the purple dust.

Wizard's Butterbeer

Butterbeer is a foaming mug of yummy, slightly alcoholic liquid that isn't as sickly-sweet as butterscotch. You can now make a fairly close replica of the alcoholic version that uses pumpkin beer or ale using this recipe.

Prep Time: 10 minutes
Serving: 1

Ingredients:
- 12 fluid ounces root beer
- 5 tablespoons butterscotch sauce
- Tablespoon of whipped topping

Directions:
1. Put the root beer in a blender and turn it up to medium speed.
2. While the blender is still running, slowly drizzle in the butterscotch sauce in a steady stream.
3. Continue to blend until everything is well incorporated.
4. Pour into a beer mug and top with the whipped topping.
5. Finally, serve and enjoy!

Love Potion Punch

This love potion is unlikely to lead to you meeting your soul mate, but you'll be too busy having fun to notice. You can use a heart-shaped cake pan instead of a Bundt pan to make the ice ring.

Prep Time: 20 minutes
Servings: 20

Ingredients:
For the ice ring:
- 16 ounces raspberries
- 8 ounces fresh pomegranate seeds
- 32 ounces boiled water, cooled
- Ice cubes

For the punch:
- 25 ounces orange juice
- 4 cups pomegranate juice
- 2 cups lemonade
- 50 ounces grape juice

Directions:
1. Arrange the berries and pomegranate seeds in a single layer in the bottom of a Bundt pan.
2. Place one layer of ice cubes on top of the berries and seeds, then pour just enough boiling water over the ice to cover it. Place the pan in the freezer for at least an hour.
3. In a punch bowl, combine all of the ingredients except the grape juice and whisk lightly.
4. When ready to serve, whisk in the grape juice and remove the ice ring from the Bundt pan.

Dragon's Heart Mocktail

This mocktail is dedicated to the brave and loyal companions of wizards—dragons. Serve this drink with blood orange slices or pink grapefruit slices as a garnish.

Prep Time: 5 minutes
Servings: 1

Ingredients:
- 3 wedges of lime
- ¾ ounce elderflower cordial
- 5 drops of lemon extract
- 1½ ounces apple juice
- ½ ounce ginger beer
- ¾ ounce agave syrup
- 1½ ounces blood orange juice
- Blood orange slice

Directions:
1. Combine the lime, cordial, and 3 drops of lemon extract in a muddle.
2. In a shaker with ice, combine the apple juice, ginger beer, syrup, and orange juice and shake vigorously.
3. Strain into a martini glass and add 2 more drops of lemon extract and a blood orange slice.

Silver-Blue Unicorn's Blood

Unicorns' blood is reported to be silver-blue and can glow in the moonlight. Even more remarkable is the fact that it's said to have the ability to keep the person who drinks it alive—even if they're an inch from death. However, whoever kills a unicorn for its blood will live a cursed and miserable life.

Prep Time: 5 minutes
Servings: 2

Ingredients:
- 2 cans 7up
- 1 teaspoon pomegranate juice
- 1 teaspoon silver cake shimmer
- 1 cup of cherry Kool-Aid
- Maraschino cherries, for garnish
- Mint leaves, for garnish
- Ice cubes

Directions:
1. Fill a jar halfway with ice.
2. Combine the 7up, pomegranate juice, and cherry Kool-Aid in a mixing glass. Stir.
3. Stir in the silver cake shimmer.
4. Serve with maraschino cherries and mint as a garnish.

Notes: Dress it up for Halloween with a unicorn cocktail pick or a creepy skull cocktail pick.

Arch Enemy Mocktail I

Like its namesake, this beverage is dark and dangerous. However, it's delicious!

Prep Time: 15 minutes
Servings: 1

Ingredients:
- 4 drops licorice extract
- ½ cup elderflower cordial
- 1 cup carbonated water
- ½ teaspoon lemon zest
- ½ teaspoon lemon juice
- 1 tablespoon dry ice

Directions:
1. In a shaker, combine the first five ingredients with ice.
2. Shake vigorously and strain into a chilled cocktail glass.
3. Finally, add the dry ice and serve.

Arch Enemy Mocktail II

The beverage is fiery and dark yet fabulous. It's presented with black ice cubes and a jalapeño slice—a perfect complement to a drink dedicated to a wizard's arch enemy.

Prep Time: 10 minutes
Servings: 1

Ingredients:
- 1 cup club soda
- 1 teaspoon tabasco sauce
- Dash of green food coloring
- 1 jalapeno pepper, thinly sliced
- Black ice cubes (made from water mixed with a dash of black food coloring)

Directions:
1. Mix the soda and tabasco together and strain into a glass. Add a dash of food coloring.
2. Serve with black ice cubes pepper slices on top.

Polyjuice Potion

Although this polyjuice potion won't help you take on someone else's appearance, it will set the tone for your wizard gathering. I like to add some dry ice to this to make it look more like a potion.

Prep Time: 5 minutes
Servings: 1

Ingredients:
- 2 ounces pomegranate juice
- ½ lime, juiced
- 2 ounces soda water
- Ginger ale, to taste
- A dash of green food coloring

Directions:
1. Combine the pomegranate juice, lime juice, and soda water in a large glass and swirl for 20 seconds.
2. Add ginger ale to taste and a dash of green food coloring. Serve with a piece of dry ice the size of an ice cube.

Blood-Sucking Bat Mocktail

Bats and bat blood are used in many wizard spells, potions, and medicine. In this recipe, the sight of blood created by the syringe injected with syrup is incredible.

Prep Time: 5 minutes
Servings: 4

Ingredients:
- 16 ounces frozen raspberries
- 2 teaspoons almond extract
- 2 ounces white sugar
- 4 ounces carbonated water
- 6 ounces club soda
- 2 ounces orange juice

Directions:
1. Puree the raspberries in a blender until smooth.
2. Press the puree through a fine-mesh sieve to separate the seeds from the pulp. The seeds should be discarded.
3. Combine the raspberry puree and white sugar in a small saucepan over medium-high heat.
4. Cook, stirring frequently, until the mixture is black and thick. This should take no more than 10 minutes.
5. Refrigerate the mixture until it's completely cooled.
6. Combine the almond extract, carbonated water, and ice in a cocktail shaker and mix vigorously for 30 seconds. Stir in the orange juice and club soda. Pour into glasses that have been cooled.
7. Before serving, fill a syringe with the raspberry syrup mixture from the pan and inject it into the mocktail.

The Dark Wizard Mocktail

When you drink this delectable cocktail, you're sipping the soul of a dark wizard, so take care! This cocktail is perfect with a licorice stick as a garnish, representing a wizard's wand.

Prep Time: 5 minutes
Servings: 1

Ingredients:
- ¾ ounce club soda
- ¾ ounce lemon juice
- ¾ ounce agave syrup
- ¾ ounce pineapple juice
- ¾ ounce apple juice
- 1-ounce lemonade
- Cola, to taste
- 1 licorice stick
- 2 drops green food coloring

Directions:
1. In a glass with ice, combine all the ingredients except for the licorice and cola.
2. Top with the cola and licorice stick as a garnish.

Just the Tonic

More discerning wizards will approve of this beverage. It's elegant and tasteful, with no hint of sweetness.

Prep Time: 20 minutes
Servings: 1

Ingredients:
- 2 ounces tonic water
- 6 ounces Earl Grey tea, chilled
- 1 dash simple syrup
- 1-ounce lemon juice
- 1 lemon, sliced
- 2 mint leaves

Directions:
1. In a large glass with ice, combine all the ingredients except the cut lemon and mint leaves and stir thoroughly.
2. Garnish with the lemon slices and mint leaves.

Black Lemonade

This intriguing-looking drink is the perfect choice for wizards who want to stay hydrated, are detoxing, or simply just celebrating with friends.

Prep Time: 5 minutes
Servings: 1

Ingredients:
- 1 lemon, juiced
- 1–2 capsules activated charcoal
- Stevia or maple syrup, to taste
- Water
- Ice cubes

Directions:
1. Cut the lemon in half and squeeze the juice out with a juicer.
2. Depending on the suggested dosage, open 1 or 2 activated charcoal capsules (check bottle or container).
3. Combine with the lemon juice in a large glass and whisk well.
4. Fill the rest of the glass with ice and water to the brim.
5. To sweeten, add 5 drops of stevia or maple syrup.

Notes: When using activated charcoal, it's critical to use enough water. Always read the package directions.

Black Magic Mocktail

Any school of witchcraft and wizardry will teach black magic with great care. This cocktail is a complicated and magical mix that'll set the mood for your wizards' party perfectly.

Prep Time: 5 minutes
Servings: 1

Ingredients:
- 1-ounce pomegranate juice
- ½ ounce balsamic reduction
- 1 ounce freshly squeezed lime juice
- 1-ounce honey infused with rosemary, thyme, and oregano
- 1-ounce grape juice
- 4 fresh raspberries

Direction:
1. In a shaker with ice, combine all of the ingredients and mix vigorously for 20 seconds.
2. Strain into an ice-filled glass.

Blood Mocktail

Drink this mocktail, and you might become as powerful as any witch or wizard! Take a sip, and see if you develop exceptional wizarding qualities. If not, at least you've tasted a delicious beverage!

Prep Time: 5 minutes
Servings: 1

Ingredients:
- 1½ ounces water
- 1½ ounces sweetened condensed milk
- 1 tablespoon chocolate syrup
- 1 teaspoon chocolate extract

Directions:
1. In a martini shaker with ice, combine all the ingredients and shake vigorously. Fill a martini glass halfway with the drink and top with cocoa beans.

"Bourbon" Butterbeer

This is a contender for any wizard's favorite drink, made with a splash of vanilla and some sweet apple juice. If you want to make the drink more visually appealing, add a spiral of apple peel.

Prep Time: 5 minutes
Servings: 4

Ingredients:
- 4 ounces butterscotch sauce
- 32 ounces apple juice
- 4 ounces water
- 8 ounces ginger beer
- 2 ounces vanilla extract
- 1-ounce butter

Garnish:
- Whipped cream
- Edible gold stars

Directions:
1. Simmer the butterscotch, apple juice, and water in a large saucepan for 5 minutes.
2. Stir in the ginger beer and cook for another 2 minutes. Remove the pan from the heat and stir in the butter and vanilla extract. Stir everything together thoroughly.
3. Pour the drink into mugs and decorate with the garnishes.

Bloody Mary Mocktail

Nothing goes better with a wizard's brunch than a bloody Mary mocktail, and this recipe makes the ultimate lazy Sunday morning tipple.

Prep Time: 5 minutes
Servings: 6

Ingredients:
- 36 ounces tomato juice
- 2 lemons, juiced
- 1 teaspoon horseradish
- ½ teaspoon Worcestershire sauce
- ½ teaspoon celery salt
- ¼ teaspoon kosher salt
- ¼ teaspoon white pepper
- 12 dashes of hot sauce (Tabasco)
- Ice cubes
- Slices of lemon, for garnish
- Celery sticks, for garnish

Directions:
1. Combine all of the first 8 ingredients in a large pitcher.
2. Add ice to 6 glasses. Divide the drink into the glasses.
3. Add celery sticks and a slice of lemon to each glass to finish the drink.

Notes: For the best impact, use a highball glass.

Pumpkin Mocktail

Pumpkins not only make a fantastic addition to drinks. They can also be used as decorations, a delicious filling for pastries and pies, or as hiding places for tiny animals!

Prep time: 5 minutes
Servings: 4

Ingredients:
For the punch:
- 7 ounces pineapple juice
- 7 ounces apple juice
- 7 ounces white grape juice
- 8 ounces orange juice
- 8 ounces lemon juice
- 8 ounces spiced syrup
- 4 ounces pumpkin puree
- 20 ounces sparkling water
- Cinnamon sticks

For the spiced syrup:
- 4 ounces demerara sugar
- 4 ounces water
- 6 whole cloves
- 6 allspice berries
- 1 cinnamon stick, broken into small pieces
- 1 star anise pod
- 6 white peppercorns
- ½ cracked nutmeg

For serving:
- Dry ice
- Hollowed-out pumpkin

Directions:
For the spiced syrup:
1. Shake the cloves, allspice, cinnamon, star anise, peppercorns, and nutmeg back and forth in a small pan over medium heat. Make sure that they don't burn.
2. As soon as the spices in the pan become fragrant and roasted, add water and sugar to the mixture. Continue to whisk until the sugar has completely dissolved.
3. Bring the mixture to a gentle simmer and then turn off the heat. Leave for another 10 minutes before removing from the stovetop.
4. Strain the syrup through a strainer and let it cool completely.

For the punch:
1. In a punch bowl safe for dry ice, combine the spiced syrup, juices, pumpkin puree, and cinnamon sticks.
2. Fill a large metal bowl with dry ice and place it inside the hollowed-out pumpkin.
3. Strain the punch into a smaller bowl than the one with the dry ice.
4. Put the punch bowl in the dry ice bowl.
5. Stir in the sparkling water to the punch.
6. To activate the dry ice, pour hot water into the metal bowl containing the ice.

Lizard Skin Mocktail

This mocktail will get your guests talking at your next get-together. The sparkling drink is bright, acidic, and has a slight bite to it.

Prep Time: 5 minutes
Servings: 1

Ingredients:
- 1-ounce pineapple juice
- 4 mint leaves
- 2 slices lime
- 3 teaspoons white sugar
- 3 ounces sparkling water

Directions:
1. Muddle the mint, lime slices, pineapple juice, and white sugar in a cocktail shaker until the sugar is dissolved.
2. Strain the cocktail into a champagne glass and top with the sparkling water and mint leaves.

Witches Blood Brew

When the dry ice in this drink is activated by liquid, it produces a fantastic, spooky vibe. Dry ice should be handled with extreme caution because it can cause burns.

Prep time: 5 minutes
Servings: 1

Ingredients:
- 8 medium blackberries
- 2 ounces agave syrup
- 2 ounces water
- 1 ounce freshly squeezed lemon juice
- 1 teaspoon maple syrup
- 5 fresh sage leaves
- 1 dash orange extract
- Blackberries, for serving
- Dry ice, for serving

Directions:
1. In a shaker, mix the berries and sage until aromatic and crushed.
2. In a cocktail shaker, combine the remaining liquid ingredients. Vigorously combine all the ingredients and pour into a glass placed in a small bowl of dry ice. Add water to the ice and serve.

Witches Brew Punch

Create a magical ambiance by serving this delectable punch at your next gathering. When poured, the emerald tint and smokey look give this drink a mysterious ambiance.

Prep Time: 5 minutes
Servings: 32

Ingredients:
- 68 ounces chilled ginger ale
- 32 ounces chilled pineapple juice
- 2½ ounces freshly squeezed lemon juice
- 128 ounces lime sherbet
- 90 ounces block dry ice
- Punch bowl that fits inside a cauldron
- Large cauldron

Directions:
1. Carefully smash the dry ice into pieces with a mallet while wearing gloves. Fill the cauldron halfway with the dry ice and keep the rest in a cooler. Soak the dry ice in the cauldron in hot water until it begins to smoke.
2. On top of the dry ice in the cauldron, place a bowl that's safe to use with dry ice. Combine the ginger ale, pineapple juice, and lemon juice in a mixing bowl.
3. Gently swirl the sherbet into the punch until it begins to melt. Serve and have fun!

Elderflower Wand Apple Martini

This mocktail will undoubtedly be a hit at your next party. I like to add some mini marshmallows to the drink for added sweetness.

Prep Time: 5 minutes
Servings: 1

Ingredients:
- 1-ounce elderflower liqueur
- 1-ounce sparkling water
- 1-ounce apple juice
- 1 tablespoon honey
- ½ lime, juiced
- Ice cubes, for serving
- Green apple slices, for serving

Directions:
1. In a cocktail shaker, combine all the ingredients except the apple slices and ice shake vigorously for 20 seconds.
2. Strain into a martini glass and add ice cubes and apple slices as a garnish.

Under the Tequila Sunrise

Whenever you need to escape the real world and experience some cocktail magic fit for any wizard, you can't go wrong with this cocktail. Serve this up to guests, and they'll, without a doubt, have a memorable drinking experience.

Prep Time: 5 minutes
Serves: 2

Ingredients:
- Ice
- 8 fluid ounces orange juice
- 4 fluid ounces silver tequila
- 1 fluid ounce grenadine
- Orange slices, for garnish
- Maraschino cherries, for garnish

Preparation:
1. Ice should be added to two tall glasses.
2. Mix the orange juice and tequila in a cocktail shaker until well combined. Pour into the two glasses.
3. Pour in the grenadine equally.
4. Garnish with an orange slice and a maraschino cherry after adding the grenadine.

Twisted Espresso Martini

This version of an espresso martini comes with a magical twist—it also contains strong coffee liqueur, PX sherry, and Amaro Nonino. The result? Intense depths of flavor that are a true knock-out.

Prep Time: 5 minutes
Serves: 2

Ingredients:
- 1¼ fluid ounces Belvedere vodka
- ¾ fluid ounce Mr. Black coffee liqueur
- ½ fluid ounce Amaro Nonino
- ¼ fluid ounce Pedro Ximénez sherry
- ¼ fluid ounce simple syrup
- Edible viola flowers, for garnish

Preparation:
1. Combine all the ingredients except the garnish in a shaker with ice and give it a good shake.
2. Strain into two chilled cocktail glasses using a fine strainer.
3. Serve with an edible viola flower as a garnish.

Bewitched Blueberry Mojito

When the sun starts to shine, sip this delightful blueberry mojito. This simple cocktail can be made in minutes with only a few ingredients.

Prep Time: 5 minutes
Serves: 6

Ingredients:
- 1 cup blueberries
- 3 lemons, chopped
- 2 tablespoons granulated sugar
- 2 mint sprigs, leaves picked
- 1½ cups white rum
- 2½ cups sparkling water

Preparation:
1. Muddle the blueberries, lemons, and sugar in a jug. The mint leaves should be bruised and added to the jug with plenty of ice.
2. Combine the rum and sparkling water and add to the jug.
3. Serve in mason jars and enjoy!

Beastly Black Russian

Vodka, coffee liqueur, and cola are used to make a traditional black Russian cocktail. Serve as a sumptuous after-dinner drink garnished with a maraschino cherry. This drink is naughty but nice!

Prep Time: 5 minutes
Serves: 1

Ingredients:
- 1½ fluid ounces vodka
- ¾ fluid ounce coffee liqueur
- Ice
- 1 maraschino cherry
- Cola to top up, chilled (optional)

Preparation:
1. Combine the vodka and coffee liqueur in a glass filled with ice and mix slowly for 30 seconds to 1 minute.
2. Serve with a cherry on top. If you want a longer drink, add a splash of cold cola.

Bergamot Mystical Mojito

In a twist on the classic mojito, fragrant bergamot zest and juice are blended with rum, mint, lime, and sugar. Serve as guests arrive for a dinner party—they'll be spellbound!

Prep Time: 20 minutes
Cook Time: 10 minutes
Serves: 6

Ingredients:
- 2 cups golden caster sugar
- 4 cups water
- 12 mint leaves
- 6 limes, juiced
- 1 bergamot orange, zested and juiced (available from ocado.com)
- 5 fluid ounces golden rum

Preparation:
1. In a medium saucepan, combine the sugar and water. Bring to a boil, then remove from the heat and cool to room temperature.
2. In a food processor, combine the mint, lime juice, and bergamot zest and juice, then add the cooled syrup and blend until blended. Pour into a plastic container and freeze, stirring every 30 minutes with a fork until completely frozen.
3. Scoop the granita into chilled glasses and pour the rum over it to serve.

Wizard's Hat Coco Fizz

Add a dash of Prosecco and a squeeze of lime to a basic coconut and rum cocktail for a festive beverage you can make in seconds. Your guests will certainly think you've donned a wizard's hat and created some magic.

Prep Time: 5 minutes
Serves: 2

Ingredients:
- 3 tablespoons coconut rum
- ½ cup coconut water
- Juice of ½ lime
- Ice
- ½ cup prosecco

Preparation:
1. In a cocktail shaker, combine the coconut rum, coconut water, and lime juice; add ice and shake until the outside of the shaker is icy-cold to the touch.
2. Serve in chilled coupe glasses with Prosecco poured on top.

Supernatural Sloe Gin

This harvest hedgerow cocktail combines botanical aromas from the gin with juniper syrup to create a sweet-sharp beverage. Wow your guests with its unique flavors.

Prep Time: 10 minutes
Cook Time: 5 minutes
Serves: 1

Ingredients:
- 3 tablespoons sloe gin
- 1½ tablespoons lemon juice
- 1½ tablespoons gin
- Ice (crushed and cubes)

For the juniper syrup
- 16 cups white caster sugar
- 7 tablespoons water
- 1 tablespoon juniper berries

Preparation:
1. Make the juniper syrup first. Combine the sugar, water, and juniper berries in a small saucepan. Bring to a boil, then remove from the heat and mash the berries gently in the liquid using a potato masher. Allow it cool completely before straining into a sterile bottle or jar. The syrup keeps for up to 2 weeks in the refrigerator.
2. In a cocktail shaker, combine the sloe gin, lemon juice, gin, and 2 teaspoons of the syrup, along with a few ice cubes. Shake well and strain into a tumbler over crushed ice. Serve right away.

Captivating Zucchini Martini

Zucchini and martini may seem like strange bedfellows, but when combined with lemon and shots of gin and vermouth, this is a delectable twist on a classic cocktail.

Prep Time: 10 minutes
Serves: 1

Ingredients:
- 1 zucchini, coarsely grated
- Juice of 2 lemons
- 2 tablespoons caster sugar
- 1½ tablespoons vermouth
- 3 tablespoons gin
- Ice
- Mint leaf, to garnish

Preparation:
1. Combine the zucchini, lemon juice, and sugar in a bowl and steep for 1 hour. Meanwhile, chill a martini glass in the refrigerator.
2. Using a strainer, strain the zucchini mixture into a jug. Fill a cocktail shaker halfway with ice, then add the zucchini syrup, vermouth, and gin. After a few gentle stirs, strain into your chilled glass. Serve with a mint leaf as a garnish.

Mischievous Mai Tai

This classic drink combines dark and white rums, vivid grenadine, triple sec, almond syrup, lime, and a vintage cherry garnish. It's the perfect brooding blend to enjoy alone or with friends.

Prep Time: 5 minutes
Serves: 1

Ingredients:
- 2 tablespoons white rum
- 2 tablespoons dark rum
- 2 tablespoons triple sec
- 1 tablespoon grenadine
- 1 tablespoon orgeat or almond syrup (we used Monin almond syrup, available online)
- Juice of ½ lime
- Maraschino cherry

Preparation:
1. In a cocktail shaker, combine all of the ingredients except the cherry and shake well.
2. Place a few ice cubes in a glass, pour in the drink, and top with a cherry.

Dreamy Driver's Punch

This alcohol-free punch is refreshing and healthful, making it ideal for designated drivers.

Prep Time: 15 minutes
Serves: 8

Ingredients:
- ¾ cup cranberries, frozen
- 7 tablespoons cranberry juice
- 2 cups blood orange juice (Sanguinello)
- Juice of 1 lime
- 8 thin wedges of lime
- 8 thin wedges of orange
- 8 mint sprigs
- 2½ cups sparkling apple juice

Preparation:
1. In a large jug (approximately 1½ gallons), combine the cranberry juice, orange juice, and lime juice.
2. Smash the frozen cranberries into shards and place them in the bottom of eight highball glasses to serve. In each glass, place a wedge of lime and orange, as well as a mint sprig, then pour in the mixed fruit juices and top up with the sparkling apple juice.

Potent Peach Punch

Add a boozy kick to your summer party with this deliciously wicked, peachy cocktail.

Prep Time: 10 minutes
Serves: 8

Ingredients:
- 4 tablespoons caster sugar
- Zest and juice of 1½ lemons
- 3 cups rosé wine
- 5 fluid ounces peach schnapps
- 1 peach, sliced
- ½ lemon, sliced
- Ice cubes
- 4 cups soda water or tonic
- Mint sprigs

Preparation:
1. Heat the sugar, lemon zest, and ½ cup of water until the sugar is completely dissolved. Allow the mixture to cool before adding it to the wine, lemon juice, and schnapps in a jug.
2. When ready to serve, fill glasses halfway with ice and fruit, add the wine mixture, then top with soda or tonic to taste. Add some mint sprigs as a garnish.

Vodka and Cranberry Blush

This drink is a cocktail with a sharp cranberry kick for a stylish dinner gathering of wizards and non-wizards alike!

Prep Time: 10 minutes
Serves: 12

Ingredients:
- 7 fluid ounces each vodka and Cointreau
- 21 fluid ounces cranberry juice
- 14 fluid ounces orange juice
- 2–3 limes
- Crushed ice, to serve

Preparation:
1. Combine the vodka and Cointreau in a jug, then add the cranberry juice and orange juice. Stir everything together thoroughly.
2. Remove the peel from 2–3 limes and cut it into strips. Pour the cocktail into 12 glasses filled with crushed ice, and finish with a strip of lime peel in each glass.

Whispering Walnut Old Fashioned

This drink is a spin on the classic cocktail, the old fashioned. It's boozy, comforting, and so good you'll want to keep the recipe a secret, only whispering it to those lucky few.

Prep Time: 10 minutes
Serves: 1

Ingredients:
- 2 fluid ounces walnut-infused whisky
- 1½ fluid ounces home-made cranberry syrup
- 2–3 dashes cinnamon bitters
- 2 cinnamon sticks
- 1 each, lemon and orange peel
- Ice

Preparation:
1. Combine the whisky, cranberry syrup, and bitters over ice in a mixing jar. Stir for around 15 to 20 seconds.
2. Invert a rock glass and smoke a cinnamon stick.
3. Fill the smoked rock glass halfway with ice and the drink.
4. Garnish with orange and lemon peels that have been burned.
5. Take a bite and enjoy!

Sorcerer's Strawberry Daiquiri

Create this chilly, strawberry-citrus slush in a blender. This drink is delicious with or without the rum—perfect for making for drinkers and non-drinkers alike.

Prep Time: 10 minutes
Serves: 8

Ingredients:
- 6 cups ice
- ½ cup white sugar
- 4 fluid ounces frozen strawberries
- ⅛ cup lime juice
- ½ cup lemon juice
- ¾ cup rum
- ¼ cup lemon-lime flavored carbonated beverage

Preparation:
1. Combine the ice, sugar, and strawberries in a blender.
2. Next, add the lime juice, lemon juice, rum, and lemon-lime soda. Blend until completely smooth.
3. Fill glasses with the mixture and serve. You can add fresh strawberries and mint as a garnish.

Brilliant Blue Hawaiian

Who says wizards and sunshine don't mix? If you want to add a tropical twist to your gathering, you can't go wrong with this striking alcoholic beverage. Garnish it with fresh pineapple slices and candied cherries, and you're sure to delight the glummest of guests!

Prep Time: 5 minutes
Serves: 1

Ingredients:
- 1 fluid ounce light rum
- 1 fluid ounce Blue Curacao liqueur
- 2 fluid ounces pineapple juice
- 1 fluid ounce cream of coconut
- 1 cup crushed ice
- 1 pineapple slice
- 1 maraschino cherry

Preparation:
1. Combine the rum, blue Curacao, pineapple juice, coconut cream, and 1 cup crushed ice in a blender; puree until smooth.
2. Pour into a highball glass that's been cooled.
3. Serve with a pineapple slice and a maraschino cherry on top.

Gleeful Grasshopper Cocktail

In a glass, this cocktail resembles a chocolate after-dinner mint. So, if you don't want to have dessert, go straight for this drink. Cheers!

Prep Time: 5 minutes
Serves: 1

Ingredients:
- ¾ fluid ounce creme de menthe
- ¾ fluid ounce white creme de cacao
- ¼ fluid ounce heavy cream
- 1 cup ice

Preparation:
1. Combine the creme de menthe, creme de cacao, cream, and ice in a cocktail shaker.
2. Cover and chill for at least an hour.
3. Fill a chilled cocktail glass halfway with the liquid.

Wonderous White Russian

The Kahlúa liqueur lends a coffee-infused touch to this classic vodka drink blended with fresh cream.

Prep Time: 5 minutes
Serves: 1

Ingredients:
- 2 fluid ounces vodka
- 2 tablespoons Kahlúa
- 1 tablespoon cream

Preparation:
1. Combine all of the ingredients in a shaker.
2. Place several ice cubes in a small glass and pour the drink over them.

Wonderful Watermelon Margaritas

My watermelon margaritas are now available in a non-frozen variant. On hot summer days, these are delicious and refreshing. Remove the tequila and replace it with a lemon-lime soda for a virgin version.

Prep Time: 10 minutes
Cook Time: 5 minutes
Serves: 4

Ingredients:
- ½ cup white sugar
- ½ cup water
- 3 strips orange zest
- 2 cups cubed seeded watermelon
- ¾ cup white tequila
- ¼ cup lime juice
- 1 pinch salt or sugar for rimming glasses
- 1 lime, cut into wedges
- 2 cups crushed ice, or as needed

Preparation:
1. In a small saucepan, bring ½ cup of sugar, water, and orange zest to a boil, stirring frequently. Cook the mixture for 3 minutes or until the sugar has dissolved. Remove the simple syrup from the heat and set it aside to cool.
2. In a blender or food processor, puree the watermelon. Pulse until the mixture is completely pureed.
3. Combine the watermelon puree, simple syrup, tequila, and lime juice in a large pitcher.
4. In a saucer, sprinkle a little salt or sugar. To wet the edge of margarita glasses, rub them with a lime slice. To rim the glasses, lightly dip the rims into the saucer and tap out any excess salt or sugar.
5. Fill the rimmed glasses halfway with crushed ice; pour the margarita mixture into the glasses; serve with lime wedges.

Captivating Caribbean Breeze

Who says wizards don't go on vacation? This is a refreshing, fruity cocktail, fit for any –on the beach or otherwise.

Prep Time: 5 minutes
Serves: 1

Ingredients:
- Ice
- 1 fluid ounce orange vodka
- 1 fluid ounce raspberry vodka
- ½ fluid ounce coconut-flavored rum
- 2 fluid ounces orange juice
- 2 fluid ounces pineapple juice
- 1 dash grenadine
- 1 orange wedge, for garnish

Preparation:
1. Ice should be added to a tall glass.
2. Over the ice, combine the orange vodka, raspberry vodka, rum, orange juice, pineapple juice, and grenadine.
3. Serve with an orange slice as a garnish.

Beguiling Beer Margaritas

Who'd have guessed that beer would be the perfect antidote to bright green margaritas? But it is! To avoid an overbearing beer flavor, consider non-micro brews. To measure the ingredients, use a limeade can, and add more water if the combination seems too sweet. Straining the pulp is always a good idea, unless you enjoy pulp, of course!

Prep Time: 5 minutes
Serves: 6

Ingredients:
- 1 (12 fluid ounces) can frozen limeade concentrate
- 12 fluid ounces tequila
- 12 fluid ounces water
- 12 fluid ounces beer
- Ice
- 1 lime, cut into wedges

Preparation:
1. Combine the limeade, tequila, water, and beer in a big pitcher. Stir until everything is thoroughly combined and the limeade has melted.
2. Garnish with lime wedges and plenty of ice. If necessary, add a little more water.

Mesmerizing Mimosa

A traditional brunch beverage, you and your friends can also enjoy this light delight on Mother's Day, Christmas, or any special occasion.

Prep Time: 5 minutes
Serves: 2

Ingredients:
- ¾ cup champagne or sparkling white wine, chilled
- ¼ cup orange juice

Preparation:
1. Combine three parts sparkling white wine and one part orange juice in a mixing glass.
2. Enjoy!

Abracadabra Baybreeze Cocktail

The Baybreeze, a spin-off of the Cape Codder, is as refreshing as any alcoholic beverage this side of the mojito. It's simple to put together but magical to taste!

Prep Time: 15 minutes
Serves: 1

Ingredients:
- 1 cup ice
- 2 fluid ounces cranberry juice
- 2 fluid ounces pineapple juice
- 1½ fluid ounces vodka
- 1 lime wedge, for garnish

Preparation:
1. Combine the ice, cranberry juice, pineapple juice, and vodka in a highball glass.
2. Serve with a wedge of lime as a garnish.

Saints and Sinners

With deep, earthy aromas and ruby color, this cocktail not only looks beautiful but tastes fantastic, too. This drink is perfect for wizards wanting a crisp, cool beverage that's the perfect balance between sweet and sour.

Prep Time: 15 minutes
Serves: 1

Ingredients:
- 2 fluid ounces vodka
- 2 fluid ounces freshly squeezed grapefruit juice
- 1 ½ fluid ounces freshly squeezed pomegranate juice
- ½ fluid ounce sweet French vermouth
- ½ ounce cream of balsamic (balsamic glaze)
- ¼ fluid ounce cold-pressed cranberry juice
- ⅛ teaspoon freshly ground pink peppercorns
- Ice cubes
- Orange zest, for garnish

Preparation:
1. Combine the vodka, grapefruit juice, pomegranate juice, vermouth, cream of balsamic, cranberry juice, and peppercorns in a cocktail shaker with some ice. Shake vigorously, then strain into a martini glass.
2. Orange zest should be sprinkled on top.

Prickly Pear Cactus Margarita

Evoking the sights and smells of faraway lands, this margarita is a fabulous addition to any party (or if you fancy a pick-me-up after a long day at work).

Prep Time: 10 minutes
Serves: 1

Ingredients:
- Coarse salt, as needed
- 2 fluid ounces tequila
- 2 fluid ounces sweet and sour mix
- 1 fluid ounce triple sec
- 1 fluid ounce lime juice
- 1 fluid ounce prickly pear syrup

Preparation:
1. Fill a small plate with salt. Wet the rim of a margarita glass and then dip it in the salt.
2. In a cocktail shaker, pour the tequila, sweet and sour mix, triple sec, lime juice, and pear syrup over ice. Shake the drink in the shaker, then strain into the prepared margarita glass.

Marvelous Mangorita

This cocktail is the perfect combination of mango and margarita. Equally delicious north or south of the border, this drink will bring a smile to any face. Serve with tasty snacks, such as tortilla chips, guacamole, and salsa.

Prep Time: 5 minutes
Serves: 1

Ingredients:
- 1½ fluid ounces tequila
- 1½ fluid ounces triple sec liqueur
- 1½ fluid ounces fresh lime juice
- 1 mango, peeled, seeded, and sliced
- 4 ice cubes
- ¼ cup mango nectar

Preparation:
1. Combine the tequila, triple sec, lime juice, mango, and ice in a blender. Blend until the ice is smashed finely.
2. To taste, sweeten with mango nectar.
3. Serve in a salt-rimmed glass with lime wedges.

Scrumptious Screwrita

Try this drink if you like margaritas. It's got the addition of orange juice, adding a zestiness, and a healthy dose of vitamin C!

Prep Time: 15 minutes
Serves: 1

Ingredients:
- ½ cup ice
- ½ cup orange juice
- 1 fluid ounce tequila
- ½ fluid ounce triple sec
- 1 teaspoon sugar
- 1 dash fresh lime juice

Preparation:
1. Add the ice to a glass.
2. Pour the orange juice, tequila, triple sec, sugar, and lime juice over the ice; stir well.
3. Add a slice of orange and some orange peel for garnish.

Captivating Classic Daiquiri

It's all about finding the correct balance in a basic daiquiri. Frozen daiquiris are wonderful, but this traditional cocktail only requires four ingredients and a cocktail shaker. Simple yet delicious.

Prep Time: 5 minutes
Serves: 1

Ingredients:
- 1 fluid ounce lime juice
- 2 teaspoons superfine sugar
- 2 fluid ounces white rum
- Ice
- Slice of lime, for serving

Preparation:
1. Combine the lime juice and sugar in a cocktail shaker.
2. Add the ice and rum and shake until thoroughly chilled.
3. Pour into a glass and garnish with a lime slice.

Ramos Gin Fizz

The frothy, velvety smoothness of the Ramos Gin Fizz cocktail is half of its fun. (The other half is its delicious taste.) It gets its trademark foamy head from an egg white and a lot of shaking (of a wand or otherwise).

Prep Time: 5 minutes
Serves: 1

Ingredients:
- 2 fluid ounces gin
- 1 egg white
- 1 tablespoon lemon juice
- 1 tablespoon lime juice
- 1 tablespoon heavy cream
- 1 tablespoon simple syrup
- 3 drops orange blossom water
- Club soda

Preparation:
1. Shake the gin, egg white, lemon and lime juice, heavy cream, simple syrup, and orange blossom in a cocktail shaker (without ice). Add the ice.
2. Shake until the ice is completely melted. Pour into a Collins glass with a splash of club soda on top. You can add a lemon slice as a garnish.

Frothing Boston Sour

A classic Boston Sour is a whiskey sour with a lovely frothy foam (created using egg whites). It not only looks beautiful but has a smooth flavor that's sure to dazzle your wizard companions.

Prep Time: 5 minutes
Serves: 1

Ingredients:
- 4 tablespoons whiskey
- 2 tablespoons fresh lemon juice
- 1½ tablespoons pure maple syrup (or simple syrup)
- 1 egg white
- Orange peel and cocktail cherry, for garnish
- Ice, for serving (optional)

Preparation:
1. Combine the whiskey, lemon juice, syrup, and egg white in a cocktail shaker with no ice. Shake it for 15 seconds.
2. Fill the cocktail shaker halfway with ice. Shake for another 30 seconds.
3. Strain the drink into a glass, allowing the froth to settle on top. If desired, serve with ice, an orange peel, and a cocktail cherry.

Tantalizing Tom Collins Cocktail

Here's how to make a traditional, tasty Tom Collins—a light and effervescent gin cocktail. To make it more aesthetically pleasing, don't forget the cherry on top!

Prep Time: 5 minutes
Serves: 1

Ingredients:
- 4 tablespoons dry gin
- 1½ to 2 tablespoons simple syrup or maple syrup
- 2 tablespoons lemon juice
- ½ cup soda water
- Ice
- Maraschino cherry and lemon wheel, for garnish

Preparation:
1. In a cocktail shaker with 4 ice cubes, combine the gin, syrup, and lemon juice. Shake vigorously until completely chilled.
2. Fill an ice-filled glass halfway with the liquid, then top it off with soda water. Serve with a lemon wheel and a cocktail cherry as a garnish.

Naughty New York Sour

The New York Sour is one of the best drinks out there, and here's how to create it. Make a traditional whiskey sour and cover it with a layer of red wine.

Prep Time: 5 minutes
Serves: 1

Ingredients:
- 4 tablespoons bourbon whiskey
- 2 tablespoons lemon juice
- 1 tablespoon maple syrup or simple syrup
- 2 tablespoons dry red wine
- Lemon twist (optional garnish)

Preparation:
1. Fill a cocktail shaker halfway with ice and add the bourbon, lemon juice, and syrup. Shake until the mixture is very cold.
2. Strain the drink into a lowball or Old Fashioned glass loaded with ice.
3. Pour the red wine over the back of a spoon, just over the drink's surface, to create a layer on top. If preferred, garnish with a lemon twist.

Mystical Moscow Mule

Because a Moscow mule is all about the ginger beer's carbonation, it's not made in a cocktail shaker. It's simply mixed directly in the cup and poured over ice to keep the carbonation.

Prep Time: 2 minutes
Serves: 1

Ingredients:
- ¼ cup vodka
- 1 tablespoon fresh lime juice
- ½ cup ginger beer
- Lime wheel or wedge, fresh mint (for garnish)

Preparation:
1. Pour the vodka, lime juice, and ginger beer into a copper mug or tumbler.
2. Add ice and a lime slice for garnish. Serve right away.

Celebratory Champagne Cocktail

Although this cocktail includes luxurious Champagne, it doesn't necessarily have to be saved for a special occasion. Indulge your naughty side, and have this drink whenever it takes your fancy.

Prep Time: 5 minutes
Serves: 1

Ingredients:
- 1 sugar cube
- 1 dash bitters
- 5 fluid ounces Champagne

Preparation:
1. Place the sugar cube into a Champagne flute.
2. Drop the bitters onto the sugar cube.
3. Fill the flute with Champagne, and don't stir it.
4. Serve and enjoy!

Apprentice's Aperol Spritz

The traditional Aperol spritz is deserving of its reputation. One of the most delightful mixed cocktails of all time, it's light and effervescent with undertones of citrus and herbs.

Prep Time: 5 minutes
Serves: 1

Ingredients:
- 4 tablespoons Aperol, chilled
- 6 tablespoons Prosecco or other sparkling wine, chilled
- 2 tablespoons soda water
- Ice (try clear ice!)
- Orange wedge and a straw, for garnish

Preparation:
1. Fill a glass halfway with ice and mix in the Aperol. Add the sparkling wine and soda water on top.
2. Serve with an orange wedge squeezed in and a gentle swirl. To avoid diluting, serve using a straw.

Charming Gin and Tonic

Here's the secret to making the perfect gin and tonic, the classic two-ingredient, botanical drink!

Prep Time: 5 minutes
Serves: 1

Ingredients:
- 4 tablespoons gin
- 8 tablespoons tonic water
- Garnish ideas: lime, lemon, cucumber, mint, orange peel, juniper berries, blood orange slice, rosemary

Preparation:
1. Fill a large cocktail or wine glass halfway with ice and whisk to chill. Any melted water should be drained.
2. Pour the gin in. Place the garnishes on top. Pour the tonic water into the glass with a bar spoon (to increase the bubbles). Serve after a quick stir.

Conjurer's Cosmopolitan Cocktail

What ingredients make up a cosmopolitan cocktail? It's not as difficult as you might imagine! This beautiful pink drink is ideal for many types of festivities.

Prep Time: 5 minutes
Serves: 1

Ingredients:
- 2 tablespoons vodka
- 2 tablespoons 100% cranberry juice
- 1 tablespoon Cointreau
- 1 tablespoon lemon juice
- 1 lime wedge
- 1 teaspoon maple syrup
- For the garnish: lime wheel (optional)

Preparation:
1. Combine the vodka, cranberry juice, Cointreau, lemon juice, and syrup in a cocktail shaker with ice. Shake for 15 seconds or until the mixture is cool. Fill a martini glass halfway with the liquid.
2. If desired, serve with a lime wedge for squeezing and a lime wheel for garnishing.

Perfect Amaretto Sour

Here's how to make the perfect amaretto sour that'll wow your guests! It's the perfect combination of amaretto, bourbon, and lemon.

Prep Time: 5 minutes
Serves: 1

Ingredients:
- 3 tablespoons amaretto
- 1 tablespoon bourbon whiskey
- 2 tablespoons lemon juice
- 1 teaspoon simple syrup or maple syrup
- 1 egg white (optional)
- 2 dashes Angostura bitters
- For the garnish: cocktail cherry or Luxardo cherry, lemon slice

Preparation:
1. In a cocktail shaker with no ice, combine the amaretto, bourbon, lemon juice, syrup, egg white, and bitters. Shake for 15 seconds.
2. Fill the cocktail shaker halfway with ice. Shake for another 30 seconds.
3. Strain the drink into a glass, allowing the froth to settle on top. Serve with a cocktail cherry and a lemon slice as a garnish.

Perfect Pomegranate Martini

The finest pomegranate martini is right here! This jewel-toned cocktail is sweet, tangy, and light, making it the ideal fruity twist on a classic cocktail.

Prep Time: 5 minutes
Serves: 1

Ingredients:
- 2 tablespoons vodka
- 2 tablespoons 100% pomegranate juice (purchased or fresh squeezed)
- 1 tablespoon Cointreau
- 1 tablespoon lemon juice
- 1 teaspoon simple syrup or maple syrup

Preparation:
1. Combine the vodka, pomegranate juice, Cointreau, lemon juice, and syrup in a cocktail shaker with ice. Shake for 15 seconds or until the mixture is cool. Pour the cocktail or martini into a cocktail or martini glass.
2. Remove a 1-inch-wide strip of lemon peel using a knife. To release the oils in the lemon peel, squeeze it into the drink. Run the peel around the edge of the glass gently before placing it in the glass and serving.

Pretty Paloma Cocktail

The typical Mexican Paloma cocktail is made with tequila and grapefruit. This zesty and refreshing cocktail is easy to create and will go down a treat on any occasion.

Prep Time: 5 minutes
Serves: 1

Ingredients:
- 4 tablespoons tequila blanco
- 4 tablespoons fresh-squeezed grapefruit juice
- 1 tablespoon fresh-squeezed lime juice
- 1 tablespoon maple syrup or simple syrup
- 2 tablespoons soda water
- Flaky sea salt and grapefruit wedge, for garnish

Preparation:
1. Make a notch in the grapefruit wedge and run it around the rim of a glass. Dip the rim's edge into a flaky sea salt plate.
2. Add the tequila, grapefruit juice, lime juice, and syrup to the glass and stir until well incorporated.
3. Fill the glass halfway with ice (transparent ice if you're feeling fancy!). Serve with a splash of soda water on top.

Classic Sidecar Cocktail

Here's how to prepare the Sidecar, one of the best traditional cocktails of all time. The ideal blend of Cognac, Cointreau, and lemon creates this sour that'll have your mouth watering with delight.

Prep Time: 5 minutes
Serves: 1

Ingredients:
- 4 tablespoons Cognac (VS or VSOP)
- 2 tablespoons Cointreau
- 2 tablespoons lemon juice
- Lemon twist or orange twist, for garnish
- Superfine sugar (optional)

Preparation:
1. Make a notch in a lemon wedge and run it around the rim of a cocktail glass. Place some superfine sugar on a plate and dip the rim of the glass in.
2. Shake all of the ingredients with a handful of ice in a cocktail shaker until chilled.
3. Pour the liquid into the prepared glass. Serve with a lemon or orange twist as a garnish.

Genius Gin Gimlet

This simple combination of peach purée and Prosecco, served in an exquisite flute, offers a terrific start to any event.

Prep Time: 10 minutes
Serves: 1

Ingredients:
- 2 fluid ounces gin
- ½ fluid ounce lime juice
- ½ fluid ounce simple syrup or pure maple syrup
- Splash of soda water (optional)

Preparation:
1. Combine the gin, lime juice, and syrup in a cocktail shaker. Fill with ice and shake until well chilled.
2. If preferred, strain into a glass and top with a splash of soda water. Serve with a lime wheel as a garnish.

Pickled Pepper Potion

At your next get-together, bring your party to life with this fiery cocktail. I prefer to serve this with some spicy pickled beans as a garnish.

Prep Time: 10 minutes
Servings: 1

Ingredients:
- 1-ounce sparkling water
- ⅓ ounce Tabasco sauce
- 1 jalapeño pepper, pickled

Directions:
1. Muddle the jalapeño pepper and Tabasco sauce in the bottom of a glass, then strain into a shot glass.
2. Add the sparkling water and a jalapeño slice to the drink as a garnish.

Conclusion

Give one of these simple recipes a try if you're searching for some innovative mocktails to serve at your next wizard's bash. (Or on your own at home!) Wannabe wizards come in all kinds, sizes, and ages, and these recipes add to the fun and excitement of practicing spells and wizardry. So, let's commemorate wizards everywhere and raise a glass of one (or a few!) of these delectable drinks. Cheers!

www.ingramcontent.com/pod-product-compliance
Lightning Source LLC
Chambersburg PA
CBHW080627170426
43209CB00007B/1533

Copyright © 2020- All rights reserved.

No part of this publication or the information in it may be quoted from or reproduced in any form by means such as printing, scanning, photocopying, or otherwise without prior written permission of the copyright holder.

This cookbook was made for Harry Potter fans by Harry Potter Fans and is not an official or authorized product. It is not approved or associated with J.K. Rowling and/or her publishers.

Harry Potter, characters, names, films, and novel features used within this book are trademarked and owned by J.K. Rowling and Warner Bros Entertainment Inc.

Appendix Measurement Conversion Chart

VOLUME EQUIVALENTS(DRY)

US STANDARD	METRIC (APPROXIMATE)
1/8 teaspoon	0.5 mL
1/4 teaspoon	1 mL
1/2 teaspoon	2 mL
3/4 teaspoon	4 mL
1 teaspoon	5 mL
1 tablespoon	15 mL
1/4 cup	59 mL
1/2 cup	118 mL
3/4 cup	177 mL
1 cup	235 mL
2 cups	475 mL
3 cups	700 mL
4 cups	1 L

WEIGHT EQUIVALENTS

US STANDARD	METRIC (APPROXIMATE)
1 ounce	28 g
2 ounces	57 g
5 ounces	142 g
10 ounces	284 g
15 ounces	425 g
16 ounces (1 pound)	455 g
1.5 pounds	680 g
2 pounds	907 g

VOLUME EQUIVALENTS(LIQUID)

US STANDARD	US STANDARD (OUNCES)	METRIC (APPROXIMATE)
2 tablespoons	1 fl.oz.	30 mL
1/4 cup	2 fl.oz.	60 mL
1/2 cup	4 fl.oz.	120 mL
1 cup	8 fl.oz.	240 mL
1 1/2 cup	12 fl.oz.	355 mL
2 cups or 1 pint	16 fl.oz.	475 mL
4 cups or 1 quart	32 fl.oz.	1 L
1 gallon	128 fl.oz.	4 L

TEMPERATURES EQUIVALENTS

FAHRENHEIT(F)	CELSIUS(C) (APPROXIMATE)
225 °F	107 °C
250 °F	120 °C
275 °F	135 °C
300 °F	150 °C
325 °F	160 °C
350 °F	180 °C
375 °F	190 °C
400 °F	205 °C
425 °F	220 °C
450 °F	235 °C
475 °F	245 °C
500 °F	260 °C